FURTHER CENTER

Other books by Yoko Danno

*

POETRY:

Epitaph for memories (The Bunny and the Crocodile Press, 2002)

The Blue Door, with James C. Hopkins (The Word Works 2006)

a sleeping tiger dreams of manhattan: poetry, photographs and sound, with James C. Hopkins and Bernard Stoltz (The IKUTA PRESS, 2008). Latvian edition, *snaudošais tīģeris sapņo par rīgu*, with illustrations by Laura Feldberga and music by Ieva Mežgaile (MANSARDS, Riga, 2012).

Aquamarine (Glass Lyre Press, 2014)

Woman in a Blue Robe (Isobar Press, 2016)

*

TRANSLATION:

Songs and Stories of the Kojiki (Ahadada Books, 2008; 2nd; revised edition, Red Moon Press, 2014)

FURTHER CENTER

Poems: 1970 ~ 1998

Yoko Danno

Introduction
Gary Snyder

Further Center

©2017 Yoko Danno

ISBN: 978-4-915813-17-7

Published by
The IKUTA PRESS

1-5-3 Sumiyoshi-yamate
Higashinada-ku, Kobe, Hyogo-ken
658-0063 Japan

http://www.ikutapress.com

Available from Amazon.com and other online stores

*

Cover design by Yoko Danno
based on the Cosmic Mandala at Simotokha Dzong
Thimphu, Bhutan

Author's portrait by Anna Walinska:
by courtesy of Rosina Rubin

In gratitude for the support of my family
throughout my life

TABLE OF CONTENTS

ACKNOWLEDGEMENTS

An earlier version of this book, *Heading for a Further Center*, which was prepared for publication in 1993, failed to appear due to the prospective publisher's financial difficulties. Since then the manuscript has been stored in a drawer of my desk. I have decided to bring it out, with 'Amarna in Snow' added, as a slightly revised, new collection, *Further Center*.

Most of the poems in this book first appeared in The Ikuta Press's annual or biennial *Anthology*, between 1972 and 1991, and in various issues (Vols. 117, 118, 119, 1975, 1977, 1978) of the *Rising Generation* (*Eigo Seinen*) published by Kenkyū-sha.

'Four Songs' (*A81*) was reprinted in *New Directions in Prose and Poetry 47* (New York: New Directions, 1983).

trilogy was first published by The Ikuta Press in 1970, as well as in *trilogy & Hagoromo: A Celestial Robe*, in 2010, by the same press.

Dusty Mirror (with doodles by David Kidd) was published in 1977 (the Ikuta Press).

'Amarna in Snow' was included in my poetry collection, *Epitaph for Memories*, published by the Bunny and the Crocodile Press in 2002.

I am deeply grateful to my departed mentors/friends: the writer David Kidd who started my writing poetry in English, Professor/poet Lindley Williams Hubbell who sustained me in my writing life from 1969 until his death in 1994 and Professor/writer Hisao Kanaseki who read all my poems and encouraged me with warm and sincere concern.

I am certainly indebted to their wise words: "Keep your mind open" (Lindley Williams Hubbell), "To create is to face the future" (David Kidd), and Hisao Kanaseki's modernistic touch, "To be is to do, *do be do be do.*"

I wish to thank from the bottom of my heart Grace Cavalieri, Doris G. Bargen, Avideh Shashaani, Hiroaki Sato and James C. Hopkins among others, whose concern for my poetry, encouragement and friendships over decades have immensely supported me and enhanced my life.

My most recent gratitude goes to Ami Kaye, the poet/editor/publisher of Glass Lyre Press who published *Aquamarine* (2014), as well as to Paul Rossiter, the poet/editor/publisher of Isobar Press who published *Woman in a Blue Robe* (2016).

Last but not least my infinite thanks go to Gary Snyder, who read my poems from time to time with warm regard, and kindly wrote the Introduction for the earlier version of this book. He encouraged me to keep up writing after my son's death, by reading the manuscript of *Amarna in Snow* in progress, from start to finish.

Yoko Danno
2017

INTRODUCTION

"Purity" is not a quality much prized these days, east or west. The old Japanese sense of purity, connected to archaic folk Shinto practices and deep cultural likes and dislikes, manifested itself − in life and art − and only occasionally − in a stunning cool lucidity − fleeting, unspotted, empty of self, poignant in its impermanence. Ms. Danno is a completely modern, urban Japanese person. Her circle of friends is artistic and academic, and includes many foreigners. Her husband is a physicist. But her sensibilities, and her research, have taken her on a journey that is personally inward, and culturally back to the mythological roots of Japan. So these poems speak out of an archetypal Japan and they hint at an essential enactment of the life of a maiden, mother, and poet.

The other side of purity is pollution. This book moves from the mind of a young woman in a chaste landscape through the fertility dances "heavy with lust" to the sweep of fundamental chemistries and energies that made the world, and some that put it all at risk. She leaves her old certainties, explores the margins, and heads out (or in) for a Further Center.

Yoko has chosen to write poetry in English rather than Japanese. She has been doing this for over 20 years. It is not that she has lived a long time out of Japan. Although she herself might not say so, I think that her choice of English is part of a strategy toward the solution of contemporary dichotomies and the unearthing of the deepest roots. If she wrote these poems in Japanese she would run the risk sounding precious or archaic. The bluntness of English is an excellent foil for her subtleties.

She got her start in a small English-language circle of American and Japanese writers which included the writer David Kidd and Hisao Kanaseki, and the remarkable American poet Lindley Williams Hubbell. The group had an extremely well-informed interest in Japanese and trans-Pacific cultural life. Mr. Hubbell had published an expert and totally contemporary book of poems, *Atlantic Triptych*, in the forties. In the early fifties he moved to Japan and later became a Japanese citizen. Mr. Hubbell has been forgotten in American literary circles, but he has continued to write and teach, to considerable avail, in Japan. He is, at this writing, 92.

These poems have craft and force. Ms. Danno has won the right to her own territory of English. They explore a range of moves, such as the linking from poem to poem that runs through the "Dusty Mirror" series, or the expansive presentation of primordial male energy in a re-telling from the Kojiki (the Japanese creation myth), in the "Yamato Takeru" play. Ms. Danno's examination of folklore, mythologies, and the language and metaphors of cosmology, geology and biology puts her on the fine edge of poetry and science.

Dualisms of ancient and modern, east and west, male and female, purity and pollution are not exactly resolved here, but each pair is illuminated in its own condition. What fine play of mind-and-language, and what an invitation to all of us to share our deepest worlds − even as we mingle cultures.

Gary Snyder
1993

* * *

TRILOGY (I)

Foreword by Lindley Williams Hubbell

1 winter journey

2 song of destruction

3 dance of fire

Foreword

"My lexicon was my only companion," wrote Emily Dickinson to the obtuse Higginson. Yoko Danno once wrote me, "I collect words from dictionaries until I come across a key word (or key words), then start choosing words again in the dictionaries to form a 'constellation' around the key word(s). I use English-English, Japanese-Japanese, English-Japanese, and Japanese-English dictionaries." Aside from this total absorption in words, there is no resemblance. Miss Dickinson's seclusion is known to all. Mrs. Iida is a young woman who lives in Kobe with her husband and their two children.

Her poetry is at once imagistic and abstract: imagist, because it consists almost entirely of images: abstract, because the coherence of the images is emotional, not discursive. The Imagist school of poets (by which of course we mean H. D.) avoided the abstract. "Go in fear of abstraction," warned their mentor, Ezra Pound. Nevertheless, in the same manifesto he called for "direct treatment of the 'thing' whether subjective or objective. " H. D. gives us direct treatment of the object: a rose, a wave. Yoko Danno gives us direct treatment of the subject: herself. H. D.'s images relate to a definite topography. Her rose blooms in a real garden, her waves crashes on a real beach. Yoko Danno's images are autonomous. They are like Marianne Moore's real toads in imaginary gardens.

This poem, with its spiritual intensity and its impeccable craftsmanship, seems to me a perfect paradigm of Mallarmé's famous dictum, "Ce n'est point avec idées, mon cher Degas, que l'on fait des vers. C'est avec des mots."

Lindley Williams Hubbell
1970

1 *winter journey*

WINTER MORNING

frost
was
broken

under the dead
leaves:

she tottered
through
the owl-howling forest,

carrying
a fox

under her numbed
arm

REST

descending from
the snow-clad
plateau,

she
made
a halt,

the wind
died,

her cheeks
aglow
with cold

REFLECTION

as usual

she
looked
in the water:

the thin
ice

screened her

from
the world

below

DAYLIGHT

the cloud broke:

the trees
cast
their netlike

shadows
upon
the crusted

snow-
field

GAME

she followed
faint
tracks

covered

with fresh
snow: a shot

heard,

the fox
winded

a wounded
bird

STORM

snowflakes
swirling,

crows
flew

into
the furious
sky

as if blown

by
the gale

SNOWBREAK

the shot
broke

the equilibrium

she
kept:

the snow
surged

into the gorge

breaking
the treacherous

ice

BLISS

hailstones
fell

filling every

depression

she left
in the snow

WINTER RAIN

the snow turned
to drizzle,

moistening

the dry
moss

in
the hollow
of an oak tree

thunder-
struck

WINTER SUN

the glazed
ground
began to thaw:

she looked
back

to shake
the dew
from her straight hair:

the pointed
trees
stood leafless against

the slippery
sky

like
a triumph

THAW

above
the lingering

snow

the bamboo grass
swayed
in the sun:

it blew
gently

with
the sweet scent

of mimosa

BREEZE

like
a stain

of blood

a camellia
fell

on
the melting
snow

as
she passed

MAGNOLIA

the air
shimmering

with
the heat

of the earth:

all
the buds

burst
into
white flame

2 song of destruction

one, a distant voice,

two, a waving hand,

three, a sorrowful face,

four, a drop of water,

five, an ant hill,

six, a stone,

seven, a trembling shadow,

eight, a flash of lightning,

nine, a broken bough,

ten, a pitfall,

eleven, a trodden path,

twelve, a fallen leaf,

thirteen, a tree

SCENE ONE: A DISTANT VOICE

all the mountains
resound
with

the shrill calls
of
birds

gathering
at
the funeral:

from
behind

the rumbling sound

of a cart
heavy
with a body, and a distant voice,

a human
cry

SCENE TWO: A WAVING HAND

the flames
still
wavering

over
the embers

of a sprawling forest

burnt
in bloom:

the hot
air

moves

like
a huge

waving hand

SCENE THREE: A SORROWFUL FACE

the earth re-
echoes
to

the sea's roar:

after
the land-

slide

the mountain
stands

in
the
shape

of a
sorrowful

face

SCENE FOUR: A DROP OF WATER

the gigantic
summits

of clouds
crumple

to a

drop
of water:

soot

falls
upon
the ruins

in heavy rain

SCENE FIVE: AN ANT HILL

the

entrances
to
an ant

hill

shrouded
by
the flow

of lava: the blind

ants

dig
their way

inward

SCENE SIX: A STONE

through
the
tight

air,

burning
and
glowing,

a stone falls

to
the
earth

at
rending

speed

SCENE SEVEN: A TREMBLING SHADOW

the wind
tears

the willow's
slender branches off

its trunk:

the ruffled
lake

reflects

a trembling
shadow

of

fear

SCENE EIGHT: A FLASH OF LIGHTNING

pregnant

clouds
gather round

the sun:

the darkening
sky

is split

by
a flash
of lightning at

birth

of
a bird

SCENE NINE: A BROKEN BOUGH

pine needles
scattered
on

the wet
sand:

the whistling
grove

distorted
till

sap oozes
from

a broken
bough

SCENE TEN: A PITFALL

the loosened

ground
caves
in

where runs

the subterranean
water: the oak-leaves vibrate

with
the distant

bay
of
hounds

at a
pitfall

SCENE ELEVEN: A TRODDEN PATH

the deep
prints

of wheels

dissolve
in the
mud:

a trodden path

fades
in
bushes, the cradle

of
dark

eggs

SCENE TWELVE: A FALLEN LEAF

a fallen
leaf

lost

in
an
eddy

of water:

the swollen
river

flows

into
the sea

for burial

SCENE THIRTEEN: A TREE

under the birdless
sky

the glare

of
the
setting

sun

stains
the
bare

hillsides along
the glassy
lake:

a tree grows

from
the
scene

of
green
carnage

3 dance of fire

1

passing through a needle's
eye

a wind

raised
incessant golden

waves

over
wheat fields

as if to set
on fire
the spikes

with
a forbidden
festival torch: the air

rolling
and curling upward

to a cypress'

top

2

the wind

trampled
the soft weeping weeds

encircling

the luminous
wavering
lake:

the flaring torches
of cannas
stirred

the dark

as silently
as the scarlet

silk
scarves

of barefoot dancers

3

coming through the sunlight
above the horizon,

spreading fan-
shaped
across the grassy

hill,

frightening
a flock of still
white birds,

a field fire

ran
on tiptoe

into
the shady woods

driven
by

a fair
wind

4

the sky aglow

as it blew
through

the blades
of pampas grass,

fanned

the smoke
of silvery flowers,

dyed

the edges
slightly carmine

as

in a
sword dance

5

breathe in, breathe out,
fill the veins
with blood,

fill the bellows
with wind

to melt the metal
to shape
the shapeless:

the seven-colored flames
in the forge
dancing

burst into

showers
of sparks

with one blow

6

the sun plunged
into
the sea,

a bolt of fire:

a breeze

sprang up,
a solo

after the chorus
in a dumb show,

blowing out
rainbows
on the spray

of sizzling waves

7

sea gulls

      sea swallows
            homeward

to the light-
house,

destroy the fire, surf-riders,

the oil-
smelling

fire

spread over the
subdued

sea

8

hills
and
mountains

in smoke, the animal-
paths

barred,

the chasing
fire

swept
over

a hole

in the
withered

grassland

9

the hydrangea
blue

deepened,

the blood
purified

in soft burning,

the
iron
wheels

rolled

over
the acid-

fruiting herbs

10

to

a reverse
world

light coming through

a pin-
hole,

the well

ran
dry,

the
oasis

nail-
marked,

a burning wind blew up,

turning the
desert

inside out

11

deep

in
the
blue

cave

eyeless
fish

felt

the warm under
current,

rocks

burning
in the dark,

ears numb with an explosion,

sulfur

into
gas

12

the guts
spurted

from
a volcano,

surging over valleys

and villages
at harvest time:

leaping
flames

caught

the festival
dancers

behind

severed
head

masks

13

before its flight

feathers
rise,

eyes gleam

over its burning
territory:

lightning pierced the eagle

to the
cliff,

the nest
smashed:

rain

washed
a dusty

mirror

DUSTY MIRROR

1 cosmosphere

2 terrasphere

3 biosphere

4 psychosphere

1 cosmosphere

1

a curved mirror

reflects

the sun's rays

in a crescent

      to a full moon

seas

dust

and mountains

diffusing the white light

the earth

shines

blue

among

stars scattered

2

scattered

light

focused

on spider's web

the earth

turns

leaving trails

of dark stars: a nebula

collapses

fusing

the

atoms

3

naked atoms

plunge

into the ocean

of hot

air

ray-showers

fall

auroras

stream

eastward

dust absorbing

the light of rolling suns

4

whirling into suns

aflame

cooling

into dark eddies

clouds

turn

in sparkling

orbits: torches topaz tornadoes

wind rises

cascades

fall

flares spurt

in violent light

5

exposed to the sun's light

piercing

the dark

nickel-iron

grains

and stones

evaporate

in showers of gold

sensitive

film holds an image

a comet

cuts in

tracing

a luminous open curve

6

a brilliant curve

forms

a golden ring

out of beads of amber light

as the moon

enters

the sun's disc

cones of shadows

move as

satellites spin

as planets roll

in lucent spheres revolving

round their glaring

nucleus

7

curling round a nucleus

spiral arms

swirl: pools

of stars

in soft shimmering clouds

the edges

of dark nebulae

reflecting

faint

light

atoms

glow

at daggers' points

8

the needle points

to the north

caught

by the earth's

magnet

the luminous wind from the sun

moves along

the curved

lines: drums

hit the air

the sound

of a silver flute

spreading out in waves

9

like waves

rippling through space

soft light

fills

the universe

sets atoms dancing

incites fast-traveling nuclei

after burst

stars

emit

hard

light

like radii

of metallic wheels

10

in the turning wheels

of luminous

clouds

stars

are born

reds lilacs amethysts greens

a brimful glass

faintly

radiates

heavy stars breathing flash

releasing gases

light

and

dust

2 terrasphere

1

elements seeds and dust
stick together

fuse into
a rolling ball

of animated
rock: the gush

cooled

falls
in dew

a core formed

the skin
crusted

sap water
oozes

from
granite

2

acid erodes granite
the wind

carries
inland

salt spray

from the breathing
sea: life

comes into being

cells
divide

wet
soil

fertilized

the water inhabited
the sky red with glow

3

in the afterglow
of the metallic

reflection
of subsiding

waves

stands
erect

a new born
island: the spiral

smoke
rises

from the vent
the dust

falling
to the ocean

bed

4

out of the abysmal bed
the burning

magma

makes its way
through strata

to a hollow: a womb
of rock: salt water

running through
fissures

veins

through mountains
the mainland

masses
deeply

rooted

5

out rooted

mountains
are worn away

by wind water and gliding
ice into deep valleys

layers
of rock

warp

to the forces
within

heat released
balance

regained
by shakes

hillsides covered
with sprouting ferns

6

ferns
flourish

at the entrance
of a cave

fungus spores blown
into the dark

tunnel: in the depth
the water

hardly moves

where blind salamanders
sleep: rock flowers

bloom on the crystalline
walls: lichens

germinate
creeping

toward light

7

in the full sunlight

needle leaf
trees

stretch their
branches

inhale: water

vapor
passes into the air

the pollen
scatters

on the swamp: circular
leaves floating

accumulate warmth

white water lilies
are in bloom

8

flowers bloom
in the rock gardens

lilies
anemones

starfish: the moon attracts

the watery
planet

the sea sways in the basins
the land swells

water circulates
through veins: fresh

undercurrents wash down
the sea shelves

leaving sediments
upon layers

of stone

9

stone
fuses

liquid

rock metamorphoses
into

crystals

under the weight
of earth: hot water

rises from
mother

magma: light
confined

in olive

green
gold

translucent sleep

10

awakening from sleep
the valley

filled

with penetrating light
before dawn

vibrates
with the deep

sound of the earth: bellbirds

burst into
song: on a cliff

human eyes

reflect

the first ray
of the sun's light

3 biosphere

1

torchlight
proceeds
meandering

through the forest
to the breast of a hill
where the flora

repeats
a flaring cycle
of buds flowers and seeds

a wind heaves
the waves
of the flickering

lake: dawn breaks
over the shooting leaves
of flowering fruit trees

the roots
extending
to a cleavage

far
below
the earth

2

rising from the dark earth
passing through rock
running between

pebbles and grains
underground
streams

cascade
into
the foaming sea

rich with
fertile eggs: hot blood
circulating

breathing the fragrant air
women dance in a ring
crushing

the soft flowering
grass beneath
their feet

deep under the soil
living water
touches heat

3

the burning heat
in the depths
urges magma upward, surging

streams of lava
filling up
cuts in the ground

a sea breeze
slackens
in the warm sunshine

alongside
the river banks
the willows sway

in a fresh green
explosion
at mating time

larks
plunge into
flowering wheat, casting

swift
shadows
of secret knives

4

knives
stuck
in the bodies, heads

hewn
the fallen
soldiers lie in the pampas

grass
after the turn
of burning wheels: the sky

ablaze
the dark area
enlarges as the planet

revolves
round the sun: at high
tide rolling above the luxuriant

grove
of seaweed
waves crush on the sunny

beach
frenzied
as in childbirth

5

like a rebirth
out of a castoff skin
water springs up

from a well
abandoned
among palm trees

under the cloudless expanse
of the blue sky: a sea
of blood red

poppies undulates, the petals
fluttering to the ground
in the summer

breeze a swarm of male bees
around a new queen
ripe for a change

migrates
to a new colony
searching for a missing unity

the sands accept skins
corpses
and flowers

6

the fruit-bearing flowers
embracing
male

organs
with pollen
fully grown in pear trees

the standing
crops
mellow for harvesting

by reapers
sickles in hands
to their ears the keen howling

of a wolf at bay
the grains threshed
ground into fine flour

a wind scatters
straw ashes
into shade

seeds
produced
in female vessels

7

through veins and vessels
sap rises
in maple trees

feeling the weakening sunlight
the leaves turn
bright red

caterpillars
into phosphorescent
butterflies

hills and fields
on fire
fuming

the transparent
blue sky: white herons
in turn

take wing
to the increasing
sound of funeral flutes

as if to slide
into a narrow path
in midair

8

high up in the air
a mistletoe
sends out roots

penetrating
the hearts
of naked boughs

an alder tree
soaring
in the slanting rays of the sun

the network
of twigs
against the glowing sky

adds
an annual ring
with the turning of the earth

crimson ivies cling
twining around
the cracked trunk

fallen leaves
fill the valley
cicadas asleep underground

9

underground
stems
store healing power

flowers killed by frost
leaf buds rest
in the branches

tight as knots
on bare trees scintillating
in the gust of cold wind

wild eyes gleam
in the darkness
beyond the wide stretch

of withered grasses
as the sun sets
lightening the deep shadows

a crescent moon
wavers
in the rippled

lake, fish
rising to bubbles
in the crystal water

10

fresh water
rising from
the deep-seated strata

wells up
stirring the clear
sand of the lake floor

sulfurous vapor
and gases purified
condensed

on rocks crystals growing
glow in the pale
morning light

young leaves unfolding
flowers breathe forth
faint perfume

vines
spiral up
marble columns

a kingfisher bathing
flashes emerald
the waves lapping on the shore

4 psychosphere

1

a castle, a mirage, offshore
in the simmering air
on the sizzling waves
that crash, splash, on rocks

a pair of crows flying
over the wet sands
the deep prints of wheels
run parallel to the sky

the sea endlessly rolling
echoes back the harsh
cries; as the sun rises
flickering loopholes

in the stone wall without
an entrance evaporate
as in a dream within
a dream fading away

at awakening moments
a dayfly quivers diffusing
light on the white gravel
of the drained valley

2

the sun fills the valley
with sudden radiance
through a rift in the clouds
as by a flash of an inward

burst, reveals dying animals
in the cavities of stumps
wounded birds in bushes
a crippled monkey astray

from its troop, tottering
across a clearing, seeking
for an entrance to a safe
haven; countless moans

cries, songs, screams
the rustle of dry leaves
merge into one hollow
sound trailing into silent

vibration in the inmost
recesses of a man's cave
an arrow of a shadow
crosses the eyes at gaze

3

quiet and fixed gaze
at the setting sun from
a hilltop, the lake water
reflecting the changeful

glow of the sky; standing
alone like a tower, its spiral
stairs ascending to a globe
of light from the skylight

a black kite soaring high
into the darkening sky
wheels through the air
last thing before the toll

once again at parting
more luminous than ever
the lucent red ball bursts
behind a passing mist

gradually declining into
the field of moonflowers
where layers of ancient cities
lie buried, the words forgotten

4

pressed and forgotten
memories rush to mind
like a jostling crowd spat
out of a subway exit

cars, antennas, electric
poles swiftly fly away
as the hot train whirls
into a long cool tunnel

keeping time with steady
setting of the sun below
the horizon, the nerves
of passengers calm down

leaving faint odors behind
a north wind dies away
white birches shed leaves
male deer their full horns

for the next growing season
wild flower plants wither
dying a deathless death
in the form of meditation

5

serenely as in meditation
lies the circular lake
surrounded by purple hills
in the last lingering light

the still surface reflects
the afterglow of the bright
burning ball transcending
its usual brilliance

in the deepening dusk
crocuses lose their colors
and gradually their forms
vanishing into darkness

night shines with dew
a breeze settles on shrubs
distant white mountains
luminously outlined

in the light of the rising
moon cleanly poised
in midair, half in shadow
half in reflected light

6

from light to light
a traveler goes roaming
trailing his own shadow
each time single-mindedly

attracted like a floating
leaf drawn toward
the quiet center
of a swirling current

to such a luminary felt
with the eyes closed, as if
filled with water seeping
from the bottom of the lake

where oysters gleam
opening and reopening
their pearl jaws like a pair
of suns emitting energy

shining beyond eyeshot
the frosted sky is alight
with a cold glow from
the fresh shimmering snow

7

darkness reflecting snow
light becomes as lucent
as the cold lake water
with silver glints of fish

swimming through weed
wavering over white smooth
pebbles; water beetles swim
round and round on the still

surface of the lake, starting
up ever-widening circles
in the hush before sunset
the afterglow turns fountains

among rocks into liquid gems
a foothold on the cliff gained
in a state free from dizziness
rises a feeling of ascending

to the sky and to the ear
accustomed to the thin air
the sound of snowflakes
falling like fragrance

8

at zero point fragrance
disperses filling the air
when waterfalls turn
into spears of ice

and mountain torrents
into solid passages
reaching out directly
to the opposite banks

independent of nutrition
the frosted trees blossom
as if shining with latent light
as if light within light gleaming

absorbing the starlight
shooting across the dark sky
at the full of the moon
the crystallizing salt lake

shines as blue as a living
planet rolling among whirling
suns as if an entrance opens
to boundless expanding space

9

reflecting blue from space
arriving through layers of air
the lake is in sweet repose
as if a union accomplished

as receptive as a deep mind
yielding like a fluid gem
full with living water flowing
in and out along the paths

of least resistance through
holes in underground rocks
through roots descending for
moisture; the earth reshapes

after a thaw; the sun rising
above the horizon, passing
through water vapor, its light
penetrating the flowering

marsh, breaks into colored
rays; water lilies appear
red, orange, yellow, turning
into flames in white light

10

not in a dream at daylight
the lake shines from within,
like a huge flower unfolding
billions of golden petals

reflecting the chain-reacting
light of the inward bursts
reveals an olive-green
island in the quiet center

like the after image
of a sun; a breeze wafting
offshore the fragrance of
a human body in the fullness

of thought; the sound
of lapping water mingles
in harmony with murmuring
voices from all quarters

as if to perfect an empty
circle a faint smile emerges
as from a depth of water
through the crystal-clear mirror

PASSAGE '77

1

an invisible shadow
       creeping on the land
              like secret ink

we have no time to lose −
storehouses burnt
the crops blighted

dust storms sweep across the roads
to the shrinking
           lake

hard cacti petrifying
bones bleaching
on the sun-baked sands

hair has gone grey and sparse −
deserts emerging in drying places
among the scanty green

"But you can't live apart from it,
you are part of it,
you live in it."

2

as the sun sets
the shadows creep across the garden –
you walk, vigilant

fearful of
a blind move
of a caterpillar crawling

unseen, unheard, silently
eating, copulating, to sleep
in its dry chrysalis

of dangling darkness
in the depth of night
you tread lightly on turf

as if in fear
of suffocating a man
buried alive under snow

in fear
of frightening
snakes coming out of the thicket

3

the wind passing through withered
trees, you hear the sound
of a waterless cascade

the sound of drifting
sands, of awakening birds
before dawn −

the wriggling and the breathing
in the darkness begin
to take form − the clapping of hands −

the sky turns a somersault −
stars and the pale
moon reflected in the water

shine above − voices, sounds
laughter amplified
vibrate in the fresh air

"Let's go and sweep the dead leaves
from the graveled paths
to the main shrine."

4 TEA CEREMONY

lanterns flicker
among the pine trees
casting breathing

shadows on the soft wet moss –
you feel the breath
of the withered

plants coming to life
in a shower –
shut off the invisible

shadow and throw
light on our way
to the tea house, maids of the unseen

host – in your slow
fluent motion as a boat
floating down the deep stream

make green tea for us –
the moon is bright, the clouds
dancing wild in the whirling wind

5 NOH DANCE

light coming through the leaves
of the sun-trees
makes a shimmering pattern

on the wooden floor −
in the slow dreamlike movement
as in crossing the rapids

the masked dancer
steps forward
toward the center

discarding the attachment
at a painful parting
for the ecstasy

of entering outer space
against the gravity of the earth
on the surf of flutes, drums and chanting −

his guide, the faint glow
of a fleeting firefly
against the dark mass of mountains

6

horns are blown, hunters set free
the hound dogs for wild
flowers still remaining in the green

time and space unleashed –
there's no boundary between you
and me, between now and then

in sharing the manifest feeling
as deep as the clear
night sky –

refreshing to feel you
in the air, in the water
in the shadow of the gigantic tree

of love, in the rising current
whirling round the quiet
center of the ever-growing vortex

"Now you can't live apart from it,
you are part of it,
you live in it."

TRILOGY （Ⅱ）

1 Hagoromo: A Celestial Robe

In the province of Ōmi, in the south of Yogo-no-sato, there is a lake called Lake Yogo. The elders of the Yogo village have handed down a story:

A long time ago, eight celestial maidens, who transformed themselves into white birds, descended from heaven and bathed at the shore of the lake. A young man, Ikatomi, saw them at a distance from the western hill and was struck by their strange beauty. He wondered if they might be celestial beings, went down to the lake, and upon seeing them close at hand, knew that they were. Ikatomi at once fell in love and could not leave them. He secretly sent his white dog to have it steal one of the celestial robes. The dog brought back the robe of the youngest, which Ikatomi hid.

The celestials became aware of their danger, and immediately the seven elder sisters flew off, but the youngest could not fly. The path to heaven was closed to her, so she stayed on the earth as a human being. (The shore, now called Kami-no-ura, Celestial Shore, is where the celestial maidens bathed.) Ikatomi married her and they lived here. She bore him two sons and two daughters. (These are the ancestors of the Ikago-no-muraji clan.) Later on, the mother found the robe and in it flew back to heaven. Ikatomi, alone in his bed, lamented.*

* * *

---

*This part is Danno's translation from a fragment of *Ōmi-no-kuni Fudoki*, a topographical work on the province of Ōmi, compiled in the early 8th century.

SCENE ONE

Where am I,
standing naked in the water,
wind gently raising ripples

ruffles the willow leaves,
my long feathers,
my long hair?

Where am I,
painful in the bright sunlight,
burning green hills overwhelming me,

lake water reflecting
a young woman,
a tremor, a fear?

Where am I from,
the sudden stir in the air,
the smell of animal,

the tumult, the clamor,
the fluttering sound of wings,
and here I am,

nowhere to hide myself,
nowhere to return,
given a new body?

What am I,
this smooth soft skin,
these pliant limbs from my body?

From thirst, hands reach out
to scoop the water −
Where is my long neck, my long bill?

My white round breast,
transformed into two small mounds
aching and swelling.

This slender waist, the breathing
belly – what are you hiding,
a slit, a split?

I feel the eyes of someone
watch me, bind me
tight to the earth.

Blow, blow, blow,
O wind, shake, roll,
let fall the burning green leaves,

rip me off the trunk,
off the roots,
take me!

SCENE TWO

1

Villagers, young and old,
flowers in their hair,
men and women in full bloom,

on foot, on horseback,
fishers and divers by water
from scattered islands

flock to the grassy slope,
the foot of the gods-residing
mountain bright in the morning sun.

"Today is our spring festival,
we celebrate the day,
our lord on his high seat

praises the fertile lake
shining, surrounded,
many-folded ranges of mountains.

"Pluck up vegetables,
gather buds and blossoms for food,
inhale the fragrant fresh air."

2

Shake, shake, shake
the golden bells in evergreen
branches, waken

the sleeping spirits, the slackening
bonfires, stamp your bare feet
on the sprouting grass,

eat and drink, sing and dance,
the full moon rising
hazy with smoke.

"My heart ruffles
like the surface of Lake Yogo
at the sight of you.

"Like waves lapping on the shore,
girls make eyes at me,
but it is you that I love.

"My heart is an island
washed by the waves of Lake Yogo,
stable and rich forever."

3

Green leaves, hair scattered,
whirling round the tall
mulberry tree, it blows

tossing, lifting, curling to the sky,
bursting, sweeping through me,
where is it from,

where to? A boat
scudding before the wind,
a bird on the wing, an arrow shot

at tearing speed,
hoofs strike, sails fill,
the taste of sweet burning body,

smell of hills and fields
being burnt for rich
ripe fruits.

The fire unknown before
sustains me in space,
no longer to fly, nor to flee.

4

Gently the blood is circulating
in my yielding body, or am I
floating, off the shore,

or the boat, unfastened,
down the meandering river?
Where am I from, where am I flowing?

Ame-ama, heaven and sea,
one at the horizon,
shimmer, glimmer, evaporate in blue.

Was it you who watched
me, who bound me?
Your staring eyes secure

me to land.
   I am sinking,
     down,
        down,
          down

deep into the soft soil,
I am the earth, your woman,
plow me and sow seeds!

SCENE THREE

1

The embers carefully kept
alive all the night —
little fires waver in the hearth

like distant memories —
of what scenes, of what world?
In the dim light come into view

the kitchen utensils —
earthen pots, pans and jars
(nuts, seeds and grains)

bottles to keep water,
pestle and mortar for brewing,
mill-stones in the nook.

Now that I have eaten food
with the people here
and drunk *sake*, of oblivion,

what am I trying to recall?
Wake up, rekindle the dying fire,
breakfast has to be cooked.

2

I am again in the bright sunlight
weeding the paddy fields,
bending my back, the wind

ruffles the young rice
shooting up from the muddy water.
Here everything is visible

in broad daylight,
no secrets, no hiding, no meaning
eyes, nothing hidden

from sight, every form
revealed, breathing,
every line clean, a carved

patterns on the earthen
jar; leaves, waves, running
water; the stretch of rice paddies,

the range of mountains, the deep
blue sky. Have I ever been up there
in my past, in my dreams?

3

Do I see all,
do I see through all, do I
see the other side of the mountains,

or the bottom of the sky?
Do I see inside
the sealed pots in storage?

What is hidden beyond
the slit of doors
in the darkness of the cellar?

Where is the wind from,
the rain, the thunder, the lightning,
the good spirits that grow

the rice in the ear waist-high,
rustling as I pass through?
Do I see the being

growing and wriggling
in my belly, strange to feel,
yet so dear to me?

4

Wet are my feet and the hem
of my ragged skirt,
I stand on a rock

amidst the sparkling
rapids of the clear stream —
ayu, shining, splash,

jerk my fishing threads —
I have climbed a long way
up the mountain path.

Are you, sweet fish, from afar
in your distant memory,
and accustomed to fresh water here,

placid among pebbles and plants,
dashing for shelter
from your own swift shadows?

Did you once belong to large
salt waters, or did I
to a larger world?

SCENE FOUR

1

Men and children out in the fields,
the head woman alone
prepares herself in the house,

cooking food with unpolluted fire,
brewing *sake* with pure water,
for the coming of yearly visiting spirits.

Shake, shake, shake
a thousand bells, encourage
bubbling gases, the blazing bonfire

where moths are swarming,
women, enhanced, dancing round,
green leaves in their hair,

in the fumes of summer grass,
"May no insects plague the crop,"
"May no storms thrash the rice plants,"

swirling to the empty height
where no wind ever blows,
no fire ever burns.

2

Reeling silk off cocoons,
I see pupas, dead
before changing into moths,

tracing back in my dim memory,
a slit — a split —
and darkness beyond.

As I sit nightly
at the loom, I hear
the fluttering sound of wings,

possibly that of a hurried flight.
Why is this untiring urge
to weave a cloth

soft as down,
light as feather,
buoyant as flying spirits,

after long toil in paddy fields,
creeping and crawling with big belly,
mowing and gleaning rice?

3

What am I looking for
in this murky mountain, besides
oak-leaves for *sake* cups, basketfuls

of fruits and berries,
acorns, nuts and mushrooms?
I have gathered enough for my family

and for the coming harvest festival
when they say spirits come
to bless us from their homeland

where ancestors live forever
in light and harmony. Overhead
white birds are flying from the north,

in the woods deer belling.
I miss what I am separated from –
Not that I love you less, my beloved,

but why this urge for flight,
this yearning for the blue sky?
Earth-bound, flesh-bound, I am split!

4

"May you descend on the holy tree,
Touch the hallowed ground,
Refresh our cleansed bodies,

"Life-giving spirits from over the sea,
Bless us with abundant crop,
Make our reed plains flourishing.

"Speak to us through the woman
dancing airily in her robe,
Be with us, eat with us, drink *sake*

with us tonight. We offer you
our first fruits, sing and dance for you
to drums, flutes, *koto*-strings,

the clapping of our hands. Descend
on us all. We purified ourselves,
our homes, our land, to receive you.

"May new life sprout from the dead,
A new sun rise from the night,
Shake, shake, shake

                    the seed-bearing bells."

SCENE FIVE

1

back
and
forth

year
by
year

shuttling
over
the snowfield

between the fine warp threads

to the arctic
zone, half-way round
the earth, on the wing in air

currents, resting on waves
at stormy night, led

by fixed
stars in mind
to the northern sky

thread
by
thread,

weaving
snow
and light

into white fabric

2

red
green
and golden

lights
swirling,
dancing wild

retreat
nowhere

the sun
stays
above the horizon

during the white summer night
of the vast thawing land

flight feathers lost
after nuptials

white birds
sit
on eggs

isolated
by the ice

on fire

in this unlighted
weaving hut

the white cloth
grows

3

as eyes look
for words
in mind

finger tips feel
for invisible markings
of plumage

white
on
white,

feather in feather

intricate patterns emerging
light-footed
dancers' steps

in right place
in right order

varied
intensified
transformed at will

at sunset
at sunrise

back and forth
between thin threads

the shuttle's
eye

gropes

4

awakened
from dreamless
sleep

on fresh mulberry leaves
worms slough off
old skins

growing whiter, translucent
transformed into pupas
in white

shelters
spun
about their bodies

exposed
to the violent
sun's rays

a link
of life-death cycle
breaks

the skilled hands
spin
the filaments

of closed
cocoons
of silk moths

into dream

SCENE SIX

1

The thick, hanging clouds break,
bare of colored leaves,
trees stick out in the snow,

the lake and the mountains
covered with woven silk,
white on white, feather in feather.

Day by day I felt within
forces brewing, for a vent
gathering, increasing, threatening —

tremor — throes — strain —
down — down — down — and a push
into the flow of light and sound.

Set fire on my parturition hut,
purge the blood and stains,
a new-born life is faltering.

Out of the blue firmament
snowflakes fluttering on the flame,
smoke softly curling into the air.

2

Shafts of golden light
stream into the weaving hut,
the sky cleared, closed white buds

unfolding, the sealed pots
in storage opened,
at waterside, white birds,

the good spirits, bathing in the sun,
ame-tsuchi, heaven and earth,
unified, made whole.

Wave slow your scarves, my children,
keep out the evil spirits,
pacify the slain.

Drawn by the invisible threads
of light, my body floats
in windless, flameless, open space.

Where am I from, where to,
dancing in the white lucent robe,
what am I, who dreams,

or is dreamt?

2 Yamato Takeru

*

Characters: Yamato Takeru, Son of Emperor Oshiro-wake
Chorus of Men (*behind the audience*)
Chorus of Women (*backstage*)

Scene: A desolate place flooded with blue-gray light.
No one is in sight.

* * *

CHORUS OF MEN
This is no-man's land
filled with harsh voices
of reed and pampas grass
where needle trees utter
sharp cries in the cold wind,
birds and beasts speak
esoteric languages.

Ashihara-no-nakatsu-kuni,
sustained between the world
above and the world below,
the Central Reed Plains
where human shadows return,
live, love and multiply.

This is a crossroads,
a twilight blue-gray zone
between night and day,
a boundary in time,
a moment in space,
where, drawn unawares,
unfulfilled hearts dance
sing and cry, craving
for what they desire.

(Enter Yamato Takeru in the form of a white bird.)

TAKERU
"Yamato
is the heart
of my country, secluded
in the mountains within mountains;
the blue-green hedges several layers deep.
How beautiful is Yamato!"   (1)

How beautiful was the mountain
I used to climb at spring festivals
to praise the land under my eyes! The air
fragrant with peach blossoms, the sky
resounding with the songs of unseen larks.

137

But where is Yamato?
I have flown from a shore
rugged with rocks,
westward to a field
muddy with withered grass,
then to this plain utterly
desolated. My mind is troubled
by a strong need.

I must find the place
to return... my home...
I have stayed away too long
from my home.

Where is Yamato?
This place is so alien that I feel
as if I were in a bad dream
within a dream. I must try to wake up
and find the way.

How have I come here? What brought me here?
It seems many things happened
in a moment's dream − I left my home
when I was sixteen.

CHORUS OF WOMEN

Your father, the Emperor, ordered you to admonish your twin
brother to attend the morning and evening banquets.

TAKERU

My brother, who had slept with the two
beautiful maidens my father had summoned
as his mistresses, was afraid.
A coward, he was.

CHORUS OF WOMEN

And you killed him early in the morning when he entered the privy
on the river.

TAKERU

I caught him, grasped him

and smashed him,
tearing off his limbs with my bare hands,
wrapped them in a straw mat
and threw them away.

People were terrified,
and my father, the Emperor, too,
when I told all this at the banquet the next morning.

CHORUS OF WOMEN
Silence fell on the table, terror spread among uncles and aunts,
brothers and sisters, and in-laws.

TAKERU
How horrifying, they murmured.
My father said to me, "There are two fierce men,
the elder and the younger Takeru of Kumaso,
in a land toward the west. They are rude
and not submissive. Therefore go and kill them."

CHORUS OF WOMEN
At that time, you still tied up your hair above your forehead like
a boy. People said you were as lovely as a girl.

TAKERU
How delighted I was
to be appointed to go to the unknown,
to subdue the savages! So glad
to be away from the genteel people
of Yamato, who nestled securely
in the green lap of beautiful mountains.

Happy to be away from those people
so easily shocked when I acted
rather than spoke,
when I revealed to them
my irresistible
dark powers!

CHORUS OF WOMEN
With the gift of your aunt, the high priestess of the Grand Shrine

of Ise whose shores are washed by successive waves from the ever-
lasting land across the sea; her own garments and a small dagger
were given to you to attach to yourself the spirit of the Sun Goddess
of Ise.

TAKERU

I set out alone for the land of Kumaso in the far west -
When I arrived at the house of Kumaso Takeru, I found
three rows of soldiers surrounding it.

A pit-dwelling was newly built and food and drinks
for the celebration feast were being prepared in excitement.
People were talking aloud about the coming festival.

When the celebration day came,
I unfastened my hair, and combed it down
like a young woman's.

Putting on the robe and skirt my aunt had given to me,
I fastened to my waist a girdle of silk, when I felt
as if a divine spell binding around me.

CHORUS OF WOMEN

You disguised yourself from head to toe as a lovely young woman.

TAKERU

I went into the house, mingled
with the women there, unsuspected.

The elder and the younger Takeru,
upon seeing me, admired me and summoned me
to sit between them.

When the feast was at its height
they bade me dance. A dark stream
slowly uncoiling within my bosom, I danced
a dance of celebration. When my eyes
met the elder Takeru's, I took out
a dagger from my bosom, and seizing
his neckband, stabbed him through the chest.

Seeing this, the younger Takeru,
overcome with fear, ran off. I chased
him to the bottom of the ladder,
seized him, stabbed him through
from the back.

In his last moments, he asked me
who I was. I said to him, "I am
the Prince of Yamato, the son
of Emperor Oshiro-wake who lives
in the Palace Hishiro and rules
the Great Eight Islands,"
and revealed my mission to him.

He understood and presented me
with the name, Brave Prince of Yamato.

CHORUS OF WOMEN
It was a proof that he recognized you to be far braver than the
two chieftains who were mightier than anybody else in the west.

TAKERU
Scarcely had I finished speaking
before I sliced him up like a ripe melon.

CHORUS OF WOMEN
Thus you slew the two rulers in the west, their men and people
surrendered and the land of Kumaso was pacified.

TAKERU
But my way back was not an easy one.
In the mountains and valleys,
in the rivers and plains, harmful
deities defied me and deluded me,
and from caves came out fierce men
with tails, Earth Spiders, blocking my way.

When I crossed the Strait of Ana, an evil
deity sent forth poisonous vapor,
suffocating me. I slew the deity,
the center of calamity there,

and thus opened up paths by water
as well as by land.

CHORUS OF WOMEN
When you entered the land of Izumo, you formed a false friendship
with the chieftain, Izumo Takeru.

TAKERU
He and I bathed together
in the Hi river, from which I came out
first, and proposed to him
to exchange our swords. I had with me
an imitation sword prepared
beforehand. Izumo Takeru came out
soon and took the imitation sword. I invited
him to cross swords, struck him
and killed him.

I made a song at his death:

"Izumo Takeru
        of the land of Izumo,
                volumes of cloud rising,

        wears a sword,
                many black vines entwined,
                        but no blade inside, alas!"   (2)

CHORUS OF WOMEN
It took you years even with your might and wit to slay or subdue all
those enemies who rebelled against the Emperor's command.

TAKERU
Clearing away thick grasses
above my head in the smoldering
mountains in the land of fire,
and struggling out of the dense fog
that shrouded me, I thought of the clear
blue sky over Yamato. I wished
I could fly... I wished to fly back
to the green lap of the lovely mountains
of Yamato, the heart of the Great Eight Islands!

But soon after I came back
from the west, the Emperor, my father,
without giving me a rest nor troops,
ordered me again to fight more battles
in the twelve lands of the east,
where unruly Emishi people
worship their local deities
who threaten the lives of strangers.

I doubted my father's intention.
I wondered if he wished me to die.

CHORUS OF MEN
You had no other choice but to obey the ordinance of the Emperor,
the head and mind of the whole nation. His will is that of the gods
and the goddesses in the Plains of High Heaven.

TAKERU
His act pure and just, his laws,
heavy on me, grated on my action
like stifling iron armor.

CHORUS OF MEN
This time the Emperor dispatched with you an adjutant and bestowed
upon you a giant spear of holly wood as a symbol of authority.

TAKERU
On my way to the eastern lands
on the Emperor's command, I again worshipped
at the court of the Sun Goddess of Ise,
the land where the divine wind blows.

CHORUS OF WOMEN
Your aunt, Princess Yamato, the high priestess of the Grand Shrine
of Ise, gave you the sword Kusanagi, and also a bag, telling you to
open it in an emergency.

TAKERU
And again I was saved by her gift.
The chieftain of the land of Sagami,
where I was passing by, asked me to kill
an extremely wild deity who lived

in the great pond in that land.

When I went into the plain to inquire,
he set fire to the grass as tall as I.

Smoke and fire surrounded me. I had no way
out. I opened the bag that had been given to me
by my aunt, and found in it
a flint and steel.

I mowed down the grass around me
with the sword Kusanagi and set a counter fire
to keep the onrushing fire away. I had
a narrow escape. I returned
and killed the chieftain and all his clan.
I burned them all.

CHORUS OF MEN
From Sagami you proceeded onto the east. While you were crossing
the sea of Running Currents, the deity of the straits raised the waves
so high −

TAKERU
Our boat, adrift like a leaf,
we could not move forward. My royal wife
Princess Oto-tachibana said:

CHORUS OF WOMEN
This must be caused by the agitated mind of the deity of the sea. I will,
in your place, go into the sea to appease his anger. You, my lord, must
complete your mission and return to the Emperor to report yourself.

TAKERU
My wife seated herself
on eight layers of straw mats,
eight layers of seal skin mats
and eight layers of silk mats
spread out on the rolling waves
and went down into the sea.

As she sank, she sang:

CHORUS OF WOMEN
"O my lord, you
standing amid the flames
on the Sagami Plain
asked after me! O my prince!"   (3)

TAKERU
Seven days later, her comb drifted ashore.
We made a tomb for her and in it placed the comb.

"O my wife, *azuma*, alas!"   (4)

Where are you now?

(Takeru dissolves in the deep blue sea. The stage becomes dark.)

CHORUS OF WOMEN
This land is the Land of Roots,
where the sun and the moon return
and shooting stars fall;
light absorbed in silence,
sound dissolved in darkness,
unstirred by storms,
untroubled by fire or ice,
unmoored human spirits come
in and out of the entrance
of a mouth-like grotto;
formless shadows sway
before taking shape
in the warm salt water
at the deep blue sea bottom.

CHORUS OF MEN
Ever drifting,
roving over sea and land,
wild plains and foggy straits,
the human mind travels far
and wide, difficult way home
through a boundary in time,
at a moment in space,
through a narrow passage of wakening,
to the Land of Root, the Land of Mother.   **145**

*(Takeru appears in human form out of the deep blue light, which
turns to pale blue-green.)*

TAKERU
What many nights I had slept
under the open sky!
What many months and years
I had spent, fight after fight,
in the eastern lands of the savage Emishi!

Then at last I went back to the house
of Princess Miyazu of the land of Owari,
whom I had promised to marry
on my return from my military mission.

I had had dangers to face, labors
imposed upon me, pacifying the unruly deities,
subduing the unsubmissive people,
in the bleak mountains and raging rivers
of the vast wild eastern lands.

How comfortable I was
with my loved one, warm and tender!
Satiated with a plenty of delicious food
and great bowls of sake she served! Then
I noticed the hem of her cloak was stained
with menstrual blood.

I sang to her:

"Across the heavenly mountain,
        Kaguyama in Yamato, fly
                long-necked swans, calling
                        keen, like sickles.
Your white arms,
        slender and pliant
                like the neck of a swan.

I wish to embrace
        your long white arms,
                I wish to sleep with

you, but on the hem
      of your long cloak
            the moon has risen."   (5)

I had kept her waiting too long. The moon
waxed and waned in vain while I was busy
fighting. That night we were married.

Next morning I set out alone,
feeling refreshed, as if reborn.
I left the sword Kusanagi and all
my belongings in my wife's bedroom.

Filled with energy and courage,
I declared I would come face to face
with the fearful deity of storm-blowing
Mount Ibuki and kill him with my bare hands.

I declared to the divine world above
and the dark world below that I would fight
for my new life. I felt myself, as if out of
old iron armor, naked and free. No!
Nobody's instrument any longer!

I went up the mountain,
where I met a white boar the size
of a bull. I took it for the messenger
of the deity. Thinking it was too easy
to beat it right away, I said aloud
I would kill it later on my way back.

At the top of the mountain, a violent
hail storm struck me. I nearly
swooned. I staggered in delirium
in the heavy storm,
through poisonous mist,
down along the mountain pass
to a spring, and rested there a while.

The clear fresh water woke me
and by and by I came to myself.

I walked further on to the plain of Tagi.
My legs swollen, my head swirling,
I walked with the help of a staff.

I had always wished to fly freely,
but where did I fail? I had always sought
after a greater and stronger power
than ever, but what failed me? My mind
flying through the blue sky, but my legs,
wobbling, wouldn't go any further.

I was as alone and fixed as a pine tree
which stood facing the land of Owari,
home of my loved one.

"On the cape of Ōtsu
        you stand alone −
                O lone pine tree,
                                my brother!
O lone pine tree,
        if you were a man,
                I would give you a sword to wear −

        I would cover you with my clothes −
                O lone pine tree,
                                my brother!"   (6)

(Takeru wakes up in the Nobono Plain. The stage becomes bright.)

TAKERU
I have found this sword
at the foot of the pine tree −

My own sword which I left behind
when I ate there on my way
to the land of Owari, to my lover's home.

I want to fight my way again with my own sword!
But my eyes can't see clearly any longer...
Where am I now? Which direction is my home...
Where is my land Yamato?... My strength is failing... failing...

"Young man whose life is full,
go wear in your hair

the fresh oak leaves of
        Mount Heguri in my land,
                    my lad!"   (7)

"Look,
white clouds are rising
from the direction of my dear old home!"   (8)

I wished to have killed
the white boar with my bare hands...
but I failed to see the true form
of the beast... I failed to confront
my true enemy... the wild...
mountain god... myself... my mind... flying...

"By the side
        of my lady's bed
                I left the sword, that sword,
                            alas!"   (9)
(The stage becomes pitch-dark.)

CHORUS OF WOMEN
Mounted messengers were sent to the Emperor to report on his death.
His wives and children in Yamato came down to the Nobono Plain
and had his tomb constructed. Crawling around in the paddy fields,
they sang, crying. Meanwhile, he was transformed into a giant white
bird, and, soaring to the sky, flew away to the beach. The wives and
children, although their feet and legs were cut by the bamboo stumps,
ran after him, forgetting their pain. They waded into the sea, weeping,
and with difficulty followed the bird that flew to the rocky shores.
From there the bird flew away to stop at Shiki in the land of Kawachi,
where they built his tomb again to calm down his spirit. The tomb is
called the Tumulus of the White Bird. Then again from that place the
bird, soaring into the sky, flew away. *

---

* The story of this one-act play with the numbered songs (1 through 9) was taken from *Songs and Stories of the Kojiki, (trans., Danno)*, compiled in the early 8ᵗʰ century, Japan.

3 Eleven-Faced Kannon

*

Avalokiteśvara:

Great One Seen Above
Who gives light to the world
Who hears the voices of suffering people

Who manifests in various forms
to save people from pain and sorrow

*

Eleven-Faced Kannon:

The three faces in front showing mercy
    give comfort to good people

The three faces at left showing wrath
    rid people of their pangs

The three faces at right showing fangs
    praise those in search of enlightenment,
    and lead them to the Buddha's teachings

The face at back, roaring with laughter
    at people in the filthy sphere, turns them
    from evil to the Buddha's ways

The face on top teaches the supreme teachings
    of the Buddha to those in the greater vehicle

* * *

1

Footmarks in the dry sand
dissolve one by one

like dying flowers
after the passing of a hot wind.

A white-robed figure
on a white elephant fading far away.

Will you wait,
will you wait a moment
and turn back?

We've followed you
a long way thirsty and dusty

limping and stumbling,
the laughter still ringing
in my head.

Why laughter,
so wild laughter

frozen now
at your back?

2

Disastrous, you may say,
irreversible, you may scold,

this land was once
bright jade green

devoid of
the debris of colored
plastics.

Can't we return
and retell the innocent, early
stories lived by our young

gods
and start again
from where we gave up,

fresh and happy,
brand new?

Get angry, if you may,
reveal your fangs,
growl!

But in the name of the goddess
of mercy,
please do not laugh!

3

Our computers foretell
by the year 2001
the earth will be crammed

with multiplying humans and nukes,
and those guided, ballistic
neutron war-headed

missiles will cloud the sky.

I shall be over 60
at the turn of the century,
used and barren.

Well, tell me a tale
that a young woman escaping love
turns into a laurel tree

long before she turns old.

Delude me,
deceive me,

conceal your fangs.

Tell us tales
freeze us as we are,

irreversible,
immortal.

4

Do it again, please,
cease the fire,

stop the chain-
reaction of fusing and splitting
atoms,

blow out the corpulent
brains —

A young woman spread herself
naked,
so I've been told,

a river
of running fire,

copulated

with a man
lurid with lust,
an elephant-headed god,

and thus destroyed
the ferocious
fire.

Was it not you,
the woman, the purifying
fire?

5

This charred
flesh
or wood,

once the image of a super
human, carved
out of a living tree,

a laurel
or a camphor tree,

what fire did it go through,
what force was in pursuit

of the holy image?
A burnt-out

torso

abandoned
in an old temple

yard,
rooted among withered
bushes and dry

stones.

6

Warriors fought to death,
towns, villages,
temples and shrines on fire.

A wartime lord besieging
his enemy's castle
attacked from behind

by surprise — a seesaw
power game
as usual.

Villagers carrying a statue
of Kannon on their backs

fled the conflagration,
took refuge in the mountains
and buried it there,

intact in the soil,

safe from pursuit —
the laughter

dissolved

into
a deep snarl.

7

We boasted of our engineering,
reshaping of nature
to our purpose,

fine works
by humans.

We cut trees, opened up
roads, covered
slopes with cement.

What's wrong with us smothering
the wild mountain gods
who have done us harm in fact?

The scarred mountains
writhe as if
in agony,

rivers rise
above their banks,

avalanches of mad
soil carry down
tons of rocks and trees,

destroying houses,
burying people. After
a footage on TV, cicadas

chirp

like a sharp rain.

8

Who can witness it all, if
in the moment after a usual
breakfast, bread, butter and coffee,

huge fire balls
suddenly
explode overhead, if

lethal rays
evaporate every
being on earth?

If our flesh blown apart
by the blast, skin hanging,
bleeding, like rags,

hair burnt, eyes
jetting out, mouth torn,
only the heart

beating, a swarm of crumbling
bodies creeping
toward a boiling river –

a smoldering woman rocking her
dead child as if to waken
it from a nightmare,

a man, arms gone,
naked, carried
by a woman in a tattered robe –

who can tell it all?

Where are you now?

Will you stop all this at once,
and reverse the scenes?
Otherwise, freeze us

as we are

and burst out
laughing,

or spare us a few moments
for a last
cry

for help,

Maya, Maria, Kannon!

9

It descended from heaven,

or sprung up
from dark masses,

on a mountain top; a sudden

revelation of hidden meaning,
the first light
of day.

It was born there
at that moment,
people used to believe,

like a child
from a woman

who became pregnant
by the sun's
golden light – It poured

on mountains, valleys,
trees, plants, birds, animals
and humans, penetrated

lakes and woods,
rivers, seas and human

minds – Where is it now,
hidden deep
within the folds

of our benumbed
brains?

10

Are we trying to bring the sun
down to the earth
in haste,

in delirium,

a violent fire ball
steadily fusing atoms, shedding light

some 93,000,000 miles away
from this watery planet,

and upon ourselves an early end,

with a peal of wild laughter
frozen?

You have come from,
or are you on your way

to the Buddha's land
5,670,000,000 years away,
and stay here

a little while
among us
everywhere, at will?

Like a lotus flower
blooming
on the filthy

muddy water
you unfold, I've heard tell,

your pure heart.

11

The sun
in a woman, the sun

goddess
of
mercy

who collects tears
of the sorrowful
in a crystal

bottle,

who saves us
from all pains and evils inside
and outside,

and brings us to happiness
if we call her name.

Do you hear us?
Do you see our mosquito cries
rising like dark clouds

from this desert?

Give us water,
a drop of your tears, please,

wait for us,
turn round,
show us

your face,

MAYA, MARIA, KANNON!

FOUR SONGS

First Song: Flight

Second Song: Diving

Third song: Six Garlands

Fourth Song: Flight

FIRST SONG: FLIGHT

Past the muddy fields, the dens, the deer, the forests,
 past the standing stones in circles,
  past the gigantic phallus,
past the plowed plains, the cultivated slopes,
 past the altars for multi-breasts
  and fat bellies,
past the pyramids, where light and shadow meet,
 past the pharaohs, the lilies, the gods-striding
  lakes fringed with papyri and reed,
past the shrines of smiling goddesses, pomegranates in hands,
  past the white marble columns, the resonant
   amphitheaters full of applauding demigods,
past the temples, the lotus, the pagodas,
    stories piled on stories,
past the churches, the cross, the spires,
    rising above the soaring towers,
past the beacons on the heights
   giving forth the magnified light
     to the violent sea
   of bloodshed battles,
past the antennas
   focusing the scattering waves of energy
    from the slumbering darkness,
past the bridges, the war monuments, the skyscrapers,
    the rocket launching-pads,
 beyond the snowfields, the crevasses, the glaciers
    slowly moving
   out of the burning depths,
  the regions of the nuclear explosion tests,
above the canyons, the rivers of thin air, the land
  of white fluffy clouds,
past the multiform mountains of vapor,
   the thick mist hiding the sun,
through the ascending and the descending currents
  against the regressing time,
through the vacuums of air-pockets,
  far above the earth's surface,
   into time outside of time,

we have flown
     into this rarefied sphere,
          where missiles carrying neutron warheads
               circulate, where old angels fear to fly,

a long turbulent journey
     since the first take-off
          from the grass-covered ground
               for the test flight without end,

fallen into this fear
     of the centrifugal force, off the earth,
          of the blind expansion,
               of the growing emptiness in suspense,

of a sudden deflation,
     of a full blown balloon bursting to pieces,
          at air-splitting, supersonic
               speed nearing the starlight,

giving ourselves to
     this frail vehicle made of thin metal
          with accurate machine mind
               shining silver reflecting the sun,

split apart by the desire
     to return half way, or to go beyond,
          threatened by the destructive power
               freed and given shape in its automatic

awakening – in dismay
     a doubt rises if we are ascending,
          or if the sky is falling on us at full speed
               like a catastrophe in an old textbook –

when we see a rainbow below,
     a feeling for a union comes back –
          if we are fading away from the core,
               or if we are heading for a further center.

SECOND SONG: DIVING

In our headlong plunging
into the expanding green darkness
through the overwhelming waves and pressure

(surging abruptly from nowhere
like sensation, fresh and untimely),
we heard a vital melody, monotonous and repeating,

of the chorus of female dancers
circling round the blossoming fruit trees
in rings of flame, their bare feet

feeling, on the soft undergrass,
the prick of the fallen needle leaves
from the shooting evergreens, their clean bodies

responding to the throbs of life
through the delicate skin of the earth
holding incandescent flows within,

the air thick with perfume
of the bright flowers fertilized with pollen,
the dazed dancers, heavy with lust,

their young breast swelling hard,
celebrate their nuptial night,
the outburst of the blind force −

multi-millions of male seeds rush,
race and meet the ripe eggs,
the hilarious joy of flesh and blood −

may our soil be rich forever,
may our crops be abundant each year,
may we be blessed with multitudinous offspring −

With a soft touch of a healer's hand
the breeze passes over the land
devastated by the unleashed force of water

swirling, overflowing, drawing us
deep into the sultry darkness,
twining, strangling us like hissing snakes,

the faceless, nameless, white-hot streams
turning inward, devouring
everything in the way — gasping for fresh air,

we struggled to rise above the surface —
our feet hit the bottom, or a rock,
and kicked — the vertical will to survive revives —

in the gray pink before delaying dawn
appear the outlines of the undulating earth,
the distant view screened by overgrown branches,

with four times forty great-grandchildren,
twice forty grandchildren and children,
the aged mother, eyes blurred, head nodding,

mumbles unclear words at her stumbling
feet, into the bare dry ground,
sterile after perpetual labor,

sinking women offer their fruits,
secretly plucked from their unhealed wounds,
to the all-swallowing high altar,

may our soil be fertile again,
may the trees bear fruit once more,
may the flowers and greens come round —

THIRD SONG: SIX GARLANDS

The tree containing her mate
             chopped to pieces, the earth
has lost her flowers and fruits,
             the ash strewn over the paths,
going back and forth through
             the slim gateway between night
and day, between life and death,
             she seeks from land to waters
for the scattered fragments of
             her son-brother-husband's body,
a long lone journey in distress
             to bring them back to the whole.

As fish break the still water,
             out of the deep shadows
human face after face emerges
             absorbing daring dreams,
took bodily form, given names,
             fly, free and uninhibited,
caught in the sun's golden net,
             gods and women, entangled,
men and goddesses, intrigued,
             hate, love and give birth,
fight, die and return to life
             on the circular blue stage.

Her sorrows and her joys sprout
             after the nightlong misty rain,
anemones drooping like wounds
             sway in the wind, coming to life
again by the touch of her hands,
             fragrant blood running in her body,
pale, isolated and alone, the mother,
             her tormented son, self-begotten
in her white womb, resting in her lap,
             in the folds of her red garment,
flower petals are falling aplenty
             like perfume as in her ascending.

The clear sun-goddess, disguised
                    as a warrior, stamping her armed feet,
confronts her wild brother-god
                    the violence, a brief peace settled,
eight children are born to them,
                    three goddesses from his snapped sword,
five gods from her crunched beads,
                    the balance broken, she withdraws,
he in excess of force intrudes into
                    her divine weaving house, violates
one of her purified women weavers,
                    causing darkness in the world below.

Black in pure white, space in the atom,
                    the fire in ice, the water in rock,
stars born through burst and fusion,
                    lakes coming after volcanic cave-in,
death, birth and growth of all creatures,
                    homes, cities, countries, universes,
the destroyer-creator-preserver held
                    in the eight-armed pliant quick body,
the three-faced god of love dancing
                    his cosmic dance in a flaring circle,
the reunion of man and woman in him,
                    in the embrace of opposing goddesses.

Through the slender body responding
                    to the cries of men, women and children,
the sick, the suffering and the dying,
                    fish, birds, animals, plants and trees,
seas, rivers, fountains and cascades,
                    sand, stones, rock, dells and mountains,
the multi-million sounds transformed
                    into golden dew in the process of thought
flow out in a voice shaking the void,
                    penetrating the deafness like laser rays
the unified man-woman holding lightly
                    a medicine bottle in its sensitive hand.

FOURTH SONG: FLIGHT

Our pilot in a hurry
    to reach the ultimate ceiling
        steered our craft sharply upward,
            his gaze fixed in the void far ahead,

through the thickening clouds
    flying blind into the thinning air,
        driven by the blast of hydrogen energy,
            as if to escape from the ghostly scenes,

the trees, over-trimmed,
    twisted, deformed and dwarfed,
        the branches cut off, the cores
            eaten away by worms, standing dead,

the flowers and the grass,
    shriveled from the impure water
        polluted by the poison from overgrown
            factories and human lust without control,

the fish afloat showing
    white bellies in the red tide,
        the birds lay eggs without hard shells,
            the animals stop breeding and yielding milk,

the sun that once dried
    the earth like parchment is now failing,
        the sky overhanging without moving clouds,
            the wind no more caressing the soft skins,

the desperate mothers
    kill their shrinking children
        before darkness gathers head,
            before they meet their premature death,

the sap rising no more
    from the roots to the tip of each leaf,
        the incandescent flows corked up find vent
            to the destructive power easily bursting out.

Once again we alight
        on the blossoming earth
                the flaming petals enclosing us
      as our feet touch the warmed soil,
           unfolding as we start
                    breathing the fragrant air.

On our journey back
        to the forgotten early ground
            where seeds were sown,
      through and beyond the dry regions,
           collecting scattered saplings
                 to bring them back to our land.

The overflow drained
        through channels underground
            to the sea for evaporation,
      the flow of energy controlled
           into golden waves of crops,
                 into purple clusters of grapes.

Ring after ring extends
        to the farthest shore, revealing
           a stone sinking onto the bottom,
      when the man and the woman embrace
           deep within each of us,
                 gracefully dancing ever after.

Once again we take off,
        driven by the brain energy,
           feeling the hands under our arms
      supporting us in the midair,
           time passing slowly through us
                 outside of swift-falling time.

As we ascend higher,
        we hear the old familiar melody
           rising from within,
      as of the sound of lapping water,
           in harmony with the chorus outside,
                 monotonous and repeating.

AMARNA IN SNOW

*It all started when I heard a voice in a dream, "Don't worry –it's Amarna."
The year before, in the summer of 1986 while scaling with his climber-
friends the Diran Peak (7,252m) in the Karakoram Himalaya, my son had
slipped off a knife-edge ridge from a height of 6,000 meters and disappeared.*
.

Since then my quest continues.

For Ryu-hei

Rays born a thousand million years ago
Crisscross the light traveling for a black
Hole a billion years ahead —

No wonder you vanished
And I'm caught here
In this fine web of light
                        <a moment>

In my memory
Happenings inter-
Mingled, shapes distorted,
Lines entangled,

Colors turned
Bluish, pink, blurred,

Into a human figure
Approaching

In a flurry
Of snow,

Silence finally found its voice.

1 Amarna

A bunch of roses was delivered to me from nowhere,
                              with no sender's name.
No petals unfurled, each stem held a pink bud,
                         a snake's head carved out of coral.

A voice said, don't worry, it's Amarna.

Pink snakes – Petrified snakes – Stone snakes –

    At the summer
    Solstice
    The sun dyed the ice
    Walls – the Grand Temple
    Of Aten
    Open to the sun

It may have happened suddenly at night –
              there ran a fissure, a tremendous surface
                    snowslide carried away
                              the climbers' dreams,

        or dreams swept away
                         by the climbers?

                    *

I was introduced to an aged man, a celebrity. He fumbled in his
pocket for his name card, in vain. Then I found his in my pocket.
He had already given it to me.

I said good-bye to him, and went downstairs. In the room on the first
floor a vase was toppled over, the flowers thrown out. I tried to put
the vase in place and the flowers back, but the floor shaking under my
feet, I couldn't stand still. The huge lamp hanging from the ceiling
was violently swinging. Then the circular building began to collapse.
The central part of the building was utterly destroyed, but I was near
the wall and missed being involved in the crush. I went out of the
ruined building.

It was unexpectedly bright outside, and people walked up and down the street as if nothing had happened.

In the darkness I could see well with my eyes close.

*

ruins
of
hopes
in
snow

a forbidden
city
on
the horizon

gleaming white
without
heat

2 *My Valentine*

Rose is a rose is a rose is a rose

My valentine…

I was going to send flowers and looked for a florist who would
make a bouquet of roses in bloom. But it turned out that the person
I intended to send it to was in great trouble. He was probably too
upset to accept my gift. I wondered if I could store this big bunch
of roses in my fridge and for how long.

I buried my letter and my family's messages
in the open crevice in ice −

Wild roses we adorned the cairn with
mountain goats devoured −

Under the deep blue sky it was blowing a gale

<a moment>

my Valentine

*

A fruit-bearing young fig tree was down and lay across the ground.
I stood it erect with a support, wishing it wouldn't bear any more
fruits until it took root firmly into the soil. I tied the support loosely
to its slender trunk so the young tree could grow full.

The wind increased gale force
On the moraine at the glacier's edge
Where the Indus is young −
A freezing rain fell on the *karakoram*,
Wetting the black stone −

My valentine is a mountain
rose, a rose, a rose, a rose −

3 The Helicopter

I had to find his body, anyway. So I got on a helicopter. My mother
and my sister were with me. But I knew nothing about the way to lift
a chopper. Before I learned the controls, it took off and hovered. In
panic I grabbed at a lever. Without knowing how, I managed to make
a landing and we got off.

I thought I had stopped the engine, but without a pilot it lifted again
and crashed into the ditch by a shop. I made for the damaged building
by myself to apologize to the shopkeeper because my mother and my
sister refused to accompany me.

Walking, I said to myself, yes, after all, I have to confront him, alone.

    What else has been lost?
    Who else survived?

The debris of the crashed chopper was neatly piled behind the sports
shop.

*

    Oh, yes, I will climb

        The cliff of blue ice
            And come face to face
                With the fearful god

        Of the wind-blowing mountain
            And destroy him
                With my bare hands −

                Where is my enemy?

4 The Roller Coaster

I was in an elevator and going up to the fifth floor
     of the apartment building where we used to live.
          A few passengers were in the cage.

I didn't know why but the floor buttons were
                         out of my reach.
     While I was desperately trying to touch a button,
          I found myself alone in a monorail car
               running along the outskirts
                   of a town.

But it was no longer a monorail car I was in,
     but a roller coaster. It shot a breakneck speed
         to the zenith and next moment
                  plunged to the bottom.

I resigned myself to it and prepared for the worst,
                   but I was no longer terrified.
     I got accustomed to being thrown up
         and down. I found the ride surprisingly
              amusing.

Then I came to the bottom of a cliff, almost vertical.
         Damn it! I said, it is absolutely impossible
   to climb this, but I was somehow on a ski lift
         and easily carried
            to the top.

Finally I arrived at our former apartment
         to take back the things I had left
             in my room,
   but it was so crowded with strangers
         I couldn't get in.

5 The Autograph

I hit back the ball, backhanded. It flew far away
                                    into the deep blue sky.
Gradually grasses came out and eventually bushes
                              covered the tennis court.
        I could barely see my opponent.

                    *

    What I had left behind was not only
    the shadow but the hair of the dead,
    and what is worse, the mortuary tablet
    ihai was nowhere to be found —

    But why is this side
    so wide apart
    from the other side?

    The grey glacier lies between —
    frozen waves, hidden crevasses under the scree —

    As the sun rises the surface
    snow begins to thaw — a bottomless
    lower world yet unrevealed —

    Worst of all, the wall
    of blue ice prevents me
    from climbing over
    into the fathomless other side —

Yet, don't worry, it's *Amarna*, the voice said,

                          Amarna in snow —

                    *

I was working together on an artwork with a young man from the other side. I found the collaboration with him pleasant. It was like playing rather than working. The young man certainly came from the other side. I asked him if I might have his autograph as a proof he was really with me. He wrote down something like a hieroglyph with brush. Now I've got positive proof, I said to myself.

The young man disappeared before I was aware of it.

*

The sun god

Aten

Sends out

Light

The hieroglyph

<Life>

At the end

Of

Each ray

6 The Heir

A tiny babe the size of a five-or-six-centimeter fish was floating in a water tank. It was alive and exquisitely built. Because I could not breast-feed it, I poured milk into the tank, wondering if this could keep it alive.

Feeling uneasy whether the baby was still alive, I revisited the aquarium. The baby had been moved to a larger tank, and his features were already a child's, and pretty too, eating food with his delicate fingers.

*

Again I heard a voice say,
      Don't worry, it's alive −

Obelisks in red granite,
      An alabaster chapel,
            Columns with flowers
                  in bud and in bloom −

The voice poured down like rays
      Of the sun streaming
              Into the inner sanctuary −

If destroyed in the making, don't worry,
                      the voice said.

7 Snakes

A basketful of snakes. I picked up one of them. It was alive and the same kind as I had received before. But, I said, that one was pink and man-made. "Don't worry, it's alright," said a man who sat on the ground, cutting the snakes into pieces before my eyes. "These are for rituals," he said, "see, each piece is moving." I wanted to watch the ritual of rebirth, but wasn't allowed to. Looking at the wriggling pieces, I felt certain they would all grow and multiply.

*

What I had left behind was not only the shadow but...

Other things to drive out of my house —
First of all the cuckoo,
Then the woodpecker,
Lastly the long-crowing cock
Of the everlasting land *Tokoyo* — For one hour,

Please, let me sleep — don't
             Wake me up so early!

                  It's long before
      Dawn — the heavenly rock gate
               is closed yet.

*

I chased a mouse and caught it. Again and again I struck at it. Bleeding, it wouldn't die easily. So I gave up beating it. I felt pity for the mouse. Doctors and nurses in white uniform surrounded me and coaxed me to drink a cup of herb tea. This is good for you, they said, this will ease your pains. But I wouldn't take it, because they said the tea might coast me my life.

*

Women, each with a bow and arrows in their hands, chased me.
I ran for my life but soon they caught up with me and surrounded
me. I crouched down there. Whatever are you going to do? The
women demanded an immediate answer of me.

*

I have no vine-woven crown,
Nor any bamboo comb,
No grapes come out, nor bamboo
Shoots sprout to hide me —

The water, oh, no, the snow
Is neck deep — I can't move any further,
Can't find shelter on this high expanse of snow,
Can't find shelter unless I close my eyes,

Close my eyes!

*

My legs swollen, my head
Swirling, I am
On the rope — I wish

I could fly!

8 Karma

The karma of the expelled

Male Deity −

He destroyed the ridges
of the heavenly paddies, filled up
the irrigation ditches with
earth, scattered about
shit and piss in a holy weaving
house, flayed a heavenly horse
from the tail up and threw it
into a bottomless

lower world −

*

I buried under the stones
A crown of wild roses,
An ice figure
Of bodhisattva, a white
Shroud priests had prepared −

Donkeys tread lightly
upon the knife edge −

And if possible, oh please
Remove this cup from here − three times
The long-crowing cock crowed −

Cowbells are ringing,
A flight of birds
Across the deep blue sky −

9 Bombardment

There was a tremendous explosion, followed by
                    flashes of light and ear-shattering sound.
I felt as if my body had gone to pieces but it was able
                    to withstand the bombardment.

                    *

I found a baby in a cave. It was deathly white. I took it up in my
arms, feeling I barely managed to be in time. But soon the head came
apart from the body. I made a desperate effort to put them together
and finally succeeded, otherwise the function of the body would have
stopped. The baby started to live again.

                    *

My son was sitting on a sunlit wooden veranda. I could see only his
clear-cut profile. He looked more serene than I had ever seen him
before. I gazed at him from the side, then suddenly everything went
black.

Alarmed I woke up. Someone had just turned off
                    the bedside lamp.

                    *

    I've got a troublesome problem on my hands −

    Give me the answer, he said.
    What is your question, I asked.
    I don't know, he said.

    I've got to make up a question
            with a definite answer by tomorrow.

            No problem
            Makasenasai

The answer is everywhere,
Anytime − for example, a flower − *gul* −

Held between pages of a notebook,
                                a mountain rose, last year.

                              *

Streams flow from the mind, uninterrupted

                                        by tranquility −

He who undergoes the utmost limit

                                of concentration −

He who travels the infinite land

                        in mind − *Bodhisattva* −

                              *

He who flashed away
            faster than light left word −
                    *<That was a dream I had dreamt
                        before I was born>*

If you must, you must − pass along
                the knife edge
                        where donkeys tread lightly

                                in scattered snow light −

A white bird a piece of
                rope in its beak

                                flying across the deep blue sky −

10 Apples

As usual I walked around in a building looking for a ladies' room.
The one I finally found was not in use. It was just repaired and
covered with plastic cloth. I walked on down a corridor, where
on both sides the walls were freshly covered with *hinoki* plywood.
It smelled good. Advancing further, I wandered into a dark area,
and finally came to a room littered with rubbish. The room was not
yet restored. I regretted having strayed into such a messy place.

Walking blindly to find an exit, finally I found myself in the open
air. Looking back, I saw a *torii*. The building seemed to be in the
precincts of a shrine. By the *torii* were placed two huge apples, red
and shiny.

In wonder I gazed at the apples. Then a strange face (that of a sun
god, I guessed) appeared in the hollow of a gigantic tree by the *torii*,
and began to eat one of the apples. I kept watching, thinking aloud,
Ah, at last one had been eaten up.

*

Tie together the ends of this severed
rope – the voice poured

into the bowels of the earth,
into the crevice,
down, deep, into the word-weaving

woman's womb
like life-giving light illuminating
the inner sanctuary

of the Grand Temple

of Aten

open to the sun.

11 The Journal

I went swimming. I stood in the filthy water knee deep. Trying
to submerge I failed, because the water was too muddy and shallow.
I waded to the middle of the river where a spring was gushing out.
The water became clear, still knee deep, but I plunged in and began
to swim.

*

Several men dressed in white stood on a balcony. Among these was
my son with that radiant smile of his. My instinct told me they were
a group of writers and journalists. Saying, this is his book, I handed
one of them a copy. I felt relieved to think that I could finally let my
son know the record of his travels in India was brought out.

*

"I hear you are going to India."
"Yes, I am."
"Why? I can't help it. I want to go."
"I'm asking you what is the reason."
*"Well, it's hard to explain, but India is calling me...I want to see
it now, I want feel it now. And moreover, I want to make sure of
something...about myself...that is yet ambiguous...."*
>
>
>
>
>
>
*.... I realized, clearly realized, that I don't have 'a song of my land,
my own song,' which is a shock to me and makes me feel sad....*

− 20th Summer

12 Laughter

The twelve-headed Goddess of mercy,
    the collector of the crystal tears
        in sorrow and pain,
            the hearer of the soundless
                voices of the suffering −

Please go away and never look back. If you
    with the fearful faces at back and sides
        turn round and show
            your merciful front,
                my resolution will waver.

I would rather cut off these threads of light,
    as the Male Deity's sacred sword
        severed the serpent *Orochi*'s
            ferocious eight heads −
                please leave the lotus flower,

            laughing wildly
                and weirdly.

          *

My son was lying on the grass, a narrow stream running between us.
He talked about his new girlfriend. I told him that his girlfriend had
married one of his friends. Things have turned out contrary to my
expectations, he said, but happenings in the mountains and in other
places were just like bubbles on a flow of water. No matter what
happened to me, I have never been lost. Of course you have not, and
the flow expands into an ocean, I said, as if I had known better.

          *

What a good time you are having,
    Singing and dancing!
        In the rock cave the Sun
            Goddess has been confined

Millenniums − the feast
　　　In supreme bliss
　　　　　　Soon to begin − the rock door

Burst open, evil spirits, myriad
　　　Voices of deities
　　　　　　Dispersed with mist − a sacred

Rope retied stretched out,
　　　You may not retreat
　　　　　　Further than this rope − laughter

Echoed like thunder, sunshine
　　　Seen between the snow-
　　　　　　Capped mountain peaks −

　　　　　　　　A glorious disk!

　　　　　　*

I got off the train as usual and went down to an underpass. As I kept
walking, suddenly the sea spread under my nose. I was somehow
floating in midair.

13 The Colosseum

The cottage was filled with mountaineers. From the windows several climbers were seen descending from the summit. When they tramped noisily into the cottage, I found them a group of *sumo* apprentices. They were naked from the waist up. The hair of some was not long enough to do up in a topknot. Their bodies were glowing with health, emanating such energy, I could feel their presence behind me.

In the center of the room was my son, talking with a somber-faced man. Their quiet attitude was in sharp contrast to the lively atmosphere around them. I joined in their conversation.

Wondering why he was here, I asked my son, "How did you come to know this gentleman?" "I met him while I was traveling, " said my son. "That's what I thought," I said. "We met in the Colosseum in Rome," the man said. "That's exactly how it should happen," I said. "I could recognize him at once," my son said, "because he had died once." I didn't know why, but again I said, "That's exactly what I thought."

*

Awakened from a long sleep

petrified snakes − pink snakes − pink flower heads

burst into bloom

in midsummer at an altitude

of 6,000 meters

<live>

brilliantly

<a moment>

My Valentine

*

Murodo, August 17, 1988

*I walked up to the ridge facing Mount Tsurugi. With me were Mr. &
Mrs. T., some alumni of the university alpine club, to which my son
had belonged, and my family. It was slightly raining all day, yet the
mountain air was refreshing. Some of the alpine plants were still in
bloom – we had a glimpse of the craggy peak of Mt. Tsurugi when
the mist momentarily cleared.*

*Near the pass over Mt. Murodo, commanding a view of Mt. Tsurugi
and the Tateyama River, we burned the garments T-san and my son
had worn during their last days. The smoke rose into the overcast sky.
Then we built a cairn, under which we buried the ashes. We inscribed
their names on one of the stones of the cairn.*

*The names of the alpine flowers: Miyama gentian, Japanese buttercup,
Hakusan primrose, Kamchatka lily, Five-petaled mountain avens*

> *Chinguruma*
> *held between pages*

> *of my notebook.*

*

I was with my son. Ah, we could meet at last, I thought. I didn't have
the feeling that he was in the world beyond and I am here. I saw him
face to face on the same plane. Hugging him, I was filled with joy.
Say what you like, I said to nobody, whatever happens to me, I would
never be afraid. He seemed to have continued mountaineering. Alone,
he said. He may be all right this time, I thought. He looks so cool
now.

"I'll keep on climbing, after all," he said.
"Of course, you may," I said.

"I saw the inscription. Thank you, Mom."

"You are alive just as I thought! Forgive me, Ryu, for writing your
name on the stone while you are still living."

He pointed to the mountain challenging him. It was craggy, black, and high. I've tried to gain the summit, for six hours, but failed, he said, and made a funny face as he used to. I'll try another route, he added.

*

Treading lightly for a land

Five billion, six hundred, seventy

million years away

from Aten's horizon in snow

Bodhisattva in white light

<smiles>

Joy -bells are ringing!

− Summer 1998
Kobe

* * *

A DREAM

A year after the accident −

A path in a gloomy wood. On one side of the path was a lane leading into the depths. The entrance to the lane was barred by a chain. From the chain a notice hung; 'You are not allowed on Saturday afternoons and Sundays.'

With a young man I went round the chain into the lane. Somehow it was understood that in the depths was the young man's mansion. While walking down the lane, I thought I would surely live with this young man.

After walking for a while between trees, we came to a clearing. It was open ground at the top of a hill overlooking a town and the sea beyond. There was no mansion, but a small raised-floor shed, only with a roof and pillars, and a few steps up to the wooden floor. No furniture was inside.

Instead of four walls, strips of cloth in five colors were hanging, gently swaying in the breeze. That was the young man's residence. On the turf around the 'shrine' many people in circles were having a picnic in the soft sunshine.

Although the land belonged to the young man, nobody seemed to care. We sat among the people on a rug spread on the grass. The young man didn't say anything, but I felt his deep sympathy for me.

Then the young man said he was studying painting and that he was going to his art school. We left the place and came to the town. As I bid farewell to him, I noticed a dictionary in his hand and suddenly realized that it was my dead son's.

− February,
1987

About the Author:

The Japanese poet **Yoko Danno** lives in Kobe. She has been writing poetry solely in English for many decades. Many of her poems have appeared in numerous international anthologies, magazines and e-journals, including *Innisfree Poetry Journal, ekleksographia, Otoliths, PINSTRIPE FEDRA, Shampoo, Big Bridge, Poetry Kanto, aglimpseof, PoetryMagazine.com, poem, home: ars poetica, Pirene's Fountain, New Directions in Prose and Poetry, Asian Cha, Tokyo Poetry Journal*, among others She is the author of several poetry books, including *Epitaph for memories, The Blue Door* (collaboration with James C. Hopkins), *trilogy & Hagoromo: A Celestial Robe* and *a sleeping tiger dreams of manhattan: poetry, photographs and sound*, by Danno, Hopkins and Bernard Stoltz. *Songs and Stories of the Kojiki* is her translation of the 8th-century compilation of Japanese myths, legends, and semi-historical accounts. Collections of her recent poems, *Aquamarine* and *Woman in a Blue Robe* were published by Glass Lyre Press and Isobar Press, respectively.

The author's portrait was drawn by Anna Walinska
in her studio in New York City in 1978.

*

~ ~ ~ ~ ~ ~ ~ ~ ~ ~

The American painter **Anna Walinska** (1906 - 1997) is known for her colorful works of the Modernist period, collages done with handmade Burmese Shan paper, portraits of well-known artists and political figures, and a large body of works in various media on the theme of the Holocaust. Works by Walinska are included in numerous public collections, most notably the National Portrait Gallery, the National Museum of Women in the Arts, the Smithsonian American Art Museum, the Denver Art Museum, the United States Holocaust Memorial Museum among others. Walinska's scrapbooks of the Guild Art Gallery, along with sketchbooks and journals on world travel are included in the Archives of American Art at the Smithsonian Institution.

~ ~ ~ ~ ~ ~ ~ ~ ~ ~

I met Anna in New York City in 1978 and 79 while I was staying in a guest apartment of the Cathedral of St John the Divine by the courtesy of Father Mann, who was then the curator of the Cathedral's gallery. He introduced me to Anna, who invited me to come to her residence/studio on Broadway. There she started drawing several portraits of me. She gave me one along with a small tableau of abstract painting, telling me it might remind me of a Japanese *sumi*-painting. I had a couple more times to meet with her; on one of the occasions she recited 'Dusty Mirror' in her drawing room with a grand piano. She was a great inspiration to me.

> "Your rabbit's ear
>> listening to a faint voice among the clamor,
>>> among the cheers and claps,
>> your eagle's eye catches on the spot
>
>> a line, a curve, an angle,
>>> tersely extracted
>>>> from baby, woman, man, child;
>
>> a color, a tone, a shade,
>>> distilled
>>>> from wind, light, waves, sounds,
>
>>> wine from grapes,
>>>> metal from ore,
>
>>>>> composing
>>>> a world
>
>>> of perfection."

$-$ *from* 'Portraits '78'

* * *

www.ingramcontent.com/pod-product-compliance
Lightning Source LLC
Chambersburg PA
CBHW020855090426
42736CB00008B/383